Shipping

~

Your Guidebook for Plans, Designs and Ideas

By David Mc Master

3. MOVING INTO A CONTAINER HOME

ISBN-13: 978-1983715426
ISBN-10: 1983715425

Introduction

In the past few years, home prices have substantially gone up. The location mostly determines the price; however, location is not the prime mover of the home price, in fact, the home itself costs a lot of money. The the average home price in the current housing market is about $300,000. Yup, that's a lot of money.

You need a lot of money to build or buy a house, and not everyone can afford it. Not having enough resources to build or buy a house did not kill people's desire to own their own house. They began to look for alternative living spaces. In the process, People came up with something interesting. The modern mind has created ideas that would have been considered silly in the past.

We are facing problems such as a failing economy and rising pollution. To add to our existing problems, population rise is also making it difficult to buy affordable land. In order to battle with these societal problems, we need to come up with eco-friendly ways of living. Interestingly, there is no end to people's creativity. In the search for affordable homes, people have come forward with interesting concepts. One of these concepts is converting shipping containers into homes. The idea to use shipping containers as homes is now getting very popular.

Shipping container homes have become the latest solution for modern and a cheaper alternative to construct homes. Often referred as cargo container architecture, or Cargotecture, they are easy to build, strong, eco-friendly and cheaper than a conventional home.

These shipping containers are used for not only creating homes but for creating coffee shops, storage space or a modular data center. Here you see a modular data center from IBM:

This is an example of a container that's used as a garden shed:

What Are Shipping Container Homes?

We are trying to live frugally, minimalistically and we do not want to consume too many resources. With this thought in mind, we are modifying our ways of living, we have learned to reuse materials.

When the word Cargotecture was coined in 2003, it was used to describe a building made fully or partially with shipping containers. Shipping containers can be used to make a low-cost home or an extravagant home, vacation home, office building or housing project.

Homes can be built easily from shipping containers because the basic structure is already present. Shipping container homes are built very fast because they can be easily moved. Since these containers are strong and can resist harsh weather, these homes are also very strong.

It is easy to modify shipping containers by cutting, welding, wiring, and plumbing. Doors can be cut, windows can be made, and rooms can be partitioned. Whether you want a studio apartment or a home with many rooms, you can easily modify the shipping containers to suit your needs. There is no restriction (technically) on what kind of house you can build. You can even stack the containers to create a multi-story house.

You can weld many containers together to create a big house in a short amount of time. Here is a container home that's stacked 3 containers high.

The shipping container architecture is on the rise for a couple of reasons: it is a wonderful way to reduce waste; it is also an ultimate solution for cheap homes. Shipping container homes are becoming a better option for temporary living as well as a permanent house. If you already have a house, you can also use a shipping container to make additional changes.

For example; This couple has a traditional house but they made an office out of shipping containers in their backyard where they could work on their architecture jobs. They paid $1800 for each container and used a crane to put them in place.

Source: https://www.youtube.com/watch?v=xqLg3Mxnqrc

Here are some benefits of using shipping container homes:

Affordable: The price of a house greatly depends on location and it's seize, however, if you are building a home from a shipping container, the average price could be just half of that. To create a spacious home, you only need three to five shipping containers. Depending on the size, shipping containers usually cost between $1800 and $5000. Some shipping containers are even available for as little as $800. You will have to pay an additional price for shipping it to your location, though.

Eco-friendly: If you want to live in an eco-friendly environment, consider this. Once the containers are considered "worn out" they will get scrapped. It costs a lot of money and energy to cut them and melt them down. Because of the cost and energy involved, shipping containers lie discarded at the port. When you build homes out of these containers, you are saving on building materials.

Fast: You can build a shipping container home pretty fast. The containers are readily available and the basic structure of the house is already present. Once the shipping containers are moved to your location, you can begin modifying them.

Strong: The shipping containers are built to resist harsh climate in the sea. thus, their structural strength is quite high.

Stacking shipping containers

A shipping container home may not be for everyone because you need to take care of a lot of things such as construction regulation in your area, weather, temperature etc. However, if you want a modern home for a small investment, it will be a very good option.

Different Types of Shipping Containers

The shipping containers ensure that the goods reach their destination safely. Depending on the type of items to be shipped, different types of containers are used. The containers vary in size and strength. Before you plan to build a house from shipping containers, you need to understand some of the common types of shipping containers that are useful for building.

Dry storage container: The most common type of shipping container. These containers are used to ship dry materials. They come in 10, 20 and 40 ft. sizes. They only have doors on one end. This is the type of container that is most used in container builds. You do have different kinds of these. You have the standard ones and the high cube variant. High cube means they are 1' 6 higher. You can find more details of the dimensions in the table below.

Tunnel container: These containers have doors on both ends. They are also called double doors containers.

Open side container: These containers come with doors that can be changed into open sides. These can be used to install big windows and sliding doors.

Refrigerated container: These containers are used to ship materials that are easily destroyed, for instance, fruits and vegetables. The temperature inside these containers is controlled. These containers are insulated and could be a good option if you would like flat walls and insulation already added.

The insulation is not very good so you will need to add some more insulation to make it energy efficient.

In the following table you can find the dimensions, weight and capacity of the most used containers.

	20' standard	40' standard	40' high cube
outside length (foot)	20'	40'	40'
outside width (foot)	8'	8'	8' 6
outside height (foot)	8'	8'	9' 6
Inside length (foot)	19' 4 1/4"	39' 5 5/8"	39' 5 5/8"
Inside width	7' 8 5/8"	7' 8 5/8"	7' 8 1/2"
inside height	7' 10 1/4"	7' 10 1/4"	8' 10 1/4"
capacity (cubic foot)	1,172	2,390	2,694
weight (pounds)	5,181	8,267	8,598

Depending on your insulation requirement of your location it would be wise to choose for the high cube variant. 20' high cube containers can be used, but they are not very common.

Cons of Shipping Container Homes

We have talked about the pro's of using shipping containers before. But let's talk about the cons of using them.

I do not want to scare you of the idea of building your container home, but these are some items to consider before planning the whole project.

Building permits: Even though shipping container architecture is becoming very popular in many places, some local authorities are still not open to shipping container homes in some areas. Steel structures are being accepted for industrial construction, however, for residential housing, steel framework is not being readily accepted. Sooner or later, this would probably change. Until then, you will have to check whether this is allowed in your area or not.

Internal temperature: Shipping containers are basically large metal boxes. Then interior temperature can be very high if not insulated. You need to spend additional money to make the internal temperature favorable by using various insulation materials. In the process, you may have to choose non-environmentally friendly solutions. Insulation also uses up the limited interior of your container home.

Health hazards: Shipping containers are not originally designed for human habitation. These containers are built using materials such as industrial paint and solvents. These substances are not good for your health. If heated to a high temperature (fire) gasses from the paint or floor epoxy will cause serious harm to your health. If paint or floor epoxy is removed without breathing protection (masks) small particles can settle down in your lungs.

If you are working on the container always use safety equipment such as safety glasses, gloves (to prevent cuts from sharp metal edges), ear protection and breathing protection (dust and welding gasses). If these containers were used to ship toxic materials, the traces might still be there. You should inform yourself what it's cargo was like before buying a container.

You can easily solve the common disadvantages associated with shipping containers. I find the pros outwit the cons.

1. Acquisition and Shipment

Where to Obtain a Shipping Container

Whether you want a home, guesthouse, garage or a shelter, the first question that will come to mind is: "Where do I obtain a shipping container?"

Obtaining a shipping container could be as simple as an online purchase or as "terrifying" as buying and moving logistics. This all depends on where you are located and your budget. If you live in a port city or a town near the port, you can easily find the containers you want. If you live far away, you will have to find the right containers and move them to your place.

In case you live near a port, you can visit the port yourself and choose the shipping containers you want. Once you have found the right containers, you can talk to the seller and buy the containers.
When you are placed very far away from the port, it might be impossible to visit the dock for inspection. In that case, you will have to look for companies that sell shipping containers. Look into the business directories and find a company near you. Call them and seal the deal.

One of the easiest ways to find shipping container is by looking into Craigslist. Before you get in touch with these sellers on Craigslist, do some research. Your research should answer the questions like: are they a registered business? Do they have a physical office? Where are they based?

Craigslist search for "shipping containers"

eBay is also a good place to buy shipping containers. Some sellers even offer free shipping if you are based in a certain area. On ebay, you can find new as well as used containers. eBay sellers offer a competitive price for shipping containers.

If you want a prebuilt tiny container house, you can get it from Amazon. Amazon offers small container homes for as less than $36000. If you want a custom-built shipping container home, you can also buy on Amazon.

Alibaba is a Chinese online store where you can find various products including shipping containers. The average price for a used container on Alibaba is $2000.

Another good option is ContainerAuction.com. Container Auction is a marketplace where shipping lines, leasing companies, and local dealers offer their container inventory to the wholesalers and retail buyers.

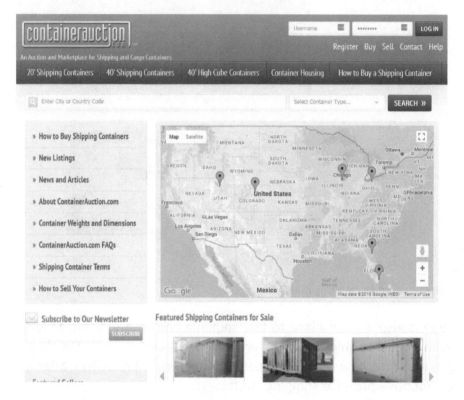

Containerauction.com

The list does not end here. You can also buy shipping containers from independent sellers. If you type "buy shipping container + your location" on Google search, you can see many websites selling new or used shipping containers, some even sell container homes.

buy shipping container + austin texas

Google Search   I'm Feeling Lucky

The local warehouses can also be a good place to buy used containers. You can save a lot of money if you visit a local warehouse and negotiate the price.

Buying a new vs used container

New shipping container does not mean the containers that are sent to you straight from the factory, instead, it is a container that has been used only once. A new shipping container is generally referred as a new "one trip container". Used containers are the containers that have been used for various purposes for several years.

No one can suggest you whether to buy a new container or a used container. What kind of container you should buy depends on your needs. In other words, what kind of container you need depends on how you are going to use the containers and your budget.

New One Trip Containers

If the highest level of quality, durability, and aesthetics are your primary concerns, you should buy a new one trip container. Get new one trip containers, if you want to build a home or office. These containers have only been used once to ship cargo from overseas. These containers are in very good condition, with a factory lock box and no signs of wear. You don't need to do any repairs to the container.

Used Containers

If the cost is your primary concern and you are also not much concerned with its beauty, used containers could be for you. Generally speaking, used containers are 8-12 years old, however, they still have a long life ahead of them. Used containers vary in color and usually have shipping logos painted on them. Used containers have dents and scratches because of rough handling. Because of these dents and scratches there can be some formation of rust on it. If you decide to buy one you should remove the rust and paint it again.

In case minimizing the cost of the container is what you want, you can look for refurbished containers, which have a long life as well as aesthetic appeal. The used containers are best for non-residential building, land-based storage for instance. These can be used as a garage, construction storage, file and record storage etc.

You can follow this rule: if you would like to save money and be prepared to give them an overhaul you can buy used ones. If you are not that handy or don't trust used containers you should buy new ones.

Never buy a used container without inspection. You should always check for the signs of wear and tear, corrosion and rust. Check the overall exterior condition, the doors, the flooring, the condition of the ceiling, and any odors. If you're not able to inspect the container because of geographic limitations, ask for pictures and inspection report from the company selling these containers.

Buying online or buying direct

Do you want to pay more for an item that you could have obtained for less? Definitely not. Will you compromise on the quality if you are going to use that item for a long time? Probably not...

Buying shipping containers online or buying direct, which one is a better option for you? It depends on a number of factors, such as:

- Pricing
- Location (where the shipping container is actually located)
- Transportation cost
- Container size and
- Container type
- New or used
- Etc...

Buying direct is the best option if the containers are available near you because you can inspect the containers. However, if you don't live in a port city or there is no port near your location, or there are no warehouses selling containers, you have to buy directly from the seller based in another city, or purchase online.

Cost involved in acquiring and shipping

How much money do you have to put in a container depends on the container type, new or used and location. When you are trying to acquire from a local warehouse, you can get a used shipping container for as little as $500-$1500.

If you are buying new containers, it might cost you anywhere between $1500 and $5000. The price of the container depends on size, type and quality.

How much you will have to pay for moving the container to your location depends on where the container is actually based. If you are buying containers from the warehouse in your town or from the port near you, the transportation charge will not be much. However, if you are buying from a seller who is hundreds, even thousands, of miles away, transportation charge might be very high. Expect to pay as much as the price of the container itself.

Permits and building codes

Sadly, you can't build a shipping container home anywhere you want.

Before you acquire containers and start building your home, there are certain things that you need to know. You have to understand zoning regulations and building codes. These are two different things. Zoning regulations will state where a house can be built. For example, a commercial building cannot be erected in the area zoned as a residential area. Building codes are the standard regulations for building houses or commercial complexes. These regulations tell how a home or commercial complex should be built. Some of the common building codes for a shipping container home are:

- The foundation types
- The minimum floor area for each room
- Minimum requirement for insulation
- Energy efficiency of your home
- Etc.

Have you built a home in the United States previously? If your answer is yes, it is very likely that you already know about the Department of Building Inspection. Just like a standard house, shipping container homes also come under the purview of Department of Building Inspection.

If you are building a container home and you don't want any problems, check what kind of building codes you have to follow. Steel is widely used in industrial construction. However, steel is not very common for residential homes. Therefore, in some regions, you might encounter problems while obtaining building permits.

In the United States, some areas are classified as 'outside of city zoning,' which refers to the area exempted from the building permit regulations. If you are located in 'outside of city zoning,' you generally don't need a permit for your container home.

Do you want to know whether there are any shipping container zoning permits and building codes in your area? The following States are considered to be the best places in the United States for shipping container homes:

Texas: There are no strict building regulations in Texas. Rural areas will be better for shipping container homes. Texas is already glutted with numerous large shipping container homes.

A container home in Dallas, Texas

California: California has strict rules for land use and new properties, however, it is also a progressive State. They approve tiny homes in certain cities. If you want a shipping container home in California, head north where the regulations are less strict.

Tennessee: Generally speaking, Tennessee is one of the freest States in the US. There are no strict building regulations. If affordability is your primary concern, look for the land in the western part of Tennessee.

Louisiana: Zoning regulations are not very strict in Louisiana, which is often touted as the number 1 for land freedom. Shipping container homes are sprouting in Louisiana.

New Orleans, Louisiana

Missouri: With the reasonable land price, warm summers and mild winters, Missouri is one of the best places to live in the United States. The State is ideal for shipping container homes because the local zoning is quite loose. You don't need building permits for shipping container homes.

Oregon: There are, of course, strict building regulations in Oregon, however, the state is also considered progressive when it comes to granting permit for alternative construction.

Alaska: Alaska is one of the best places in the United States for container homes. There are already many cargo homes in Alaska.

Perhaps, you are not in the US, but in **Canada**. Canada has different regulations. In Canada, the Building Code defines shipping containers as structures. Therefore, shipping container homes are subject to the same regulations as traditional buildings. If you want to place a shipping container on the residential area, you must provide the building department with a written description of how you intend to use it.

Here is my little disclaimer: Always check with your local department of building inspection before building your home. Otherwise you could be in for a surprise.

How long will it last?

The average life of a residential home is thought to be 40 years. You might ask, will the shipping container home last as long as a standard home?

In order to answer the question, we have to consider a couple of things, such as:

- Is it a new container or used?
- What's the condition of the used container?
- Did you remove the corrosion on the container?
- Did you paint it?
- Do you do regular checks?
- What kind of material did you use?
- Were your doors and windows properly installed?

What about rust and corrosion? Won't a metal shipping container rust quite easily?

A shipping container is made from non-corrosive Corten steel. The word corten comes from "**cor**rosion resistance and **ten**sile strength". If you have a "naked" corten steel container (without paint) it would begin to rust. The special ability of corten steel that it creates a layer of corrosion that protects the other steel from rusting.

The steel creates its own coating in the form of corrosion, this is called "weathering". Technically you could expose your container to the weather to create the "corrosion look", but you would have to remove all the paint. My advice would be to remove any rust spots and paint over it. Paint is also used to control temperature inside the container (see later chapter).

2. The Building Process

Finding a contractor or doing it yourself

Already dreaming about having a container home? Now it's the time to walk into the design process and customization of shipping containers. There are three options for you:

- Get a prebuilt shipping container home
- Find a contractor and ask him to build a container home
- Build one yourself

Prebuilt shipping container homes
If you do not want to take the troubles of designing and customization, you can directly buy prebuilt shipping container homes. A simple Google search will help you find the marketplaces for prebuilt container homes.

Find a contractor and ask him to build a container home.
Building your own home, whether it is a traditional home or a container home, is very rewarding. However, building your own shipping container home is not a viable option for everyone. If you do not have any experience and knowledge, it can cost you a lot. In that case, finding a contractor and asking him to build a container home for you is the best option. If you want to hire a contractor, find contractors with experience.

Do some research and try to find one in your area. Talk to the people who have already built container homes and ask for recommendations. If there are no contractors who have expertise in building container homes, don't think that your dreams have shattered. Look online and try to find agencies or independent contractor who build container homes.

Building one yourself

Building your home from a steel boxes is hard work; however, it can be one of the most rewarding experiences of your life. If saving money and being creative is on your priority list, you can try this option. Building one yourself will give you a lot of freedom to make the home of your choice.

Build a container home on a budget

It starts with the size. What kind of house do you want, a tiny house made from a single container, or a big home made by stacking and aligning multiple containers? The common sizes of the containers are 20 feet by 8 feet and 40 feet by 8 feet. The smaller sized containers will give you the floor area of about 160 square feet and the larger container will give 320 square feet living area. Don't forget that some of it will be used up for insulation.

The second stage of building a container home is determining the cost. How much budget do you have for your house? If you are buying a prebuilt small home, you can get it for around $40,000, and pay few more thousands to deliver the home to your location. If you are building a large container home, it can cost you as much as $200,000, which is still less than some traditional homes.

Once you have determined the size of the home, start making the plans for the foundation, floor, roof, doors and windows (you will have to cut the frames), insulation, installing utilities, painting, and decoration.

Purchasing the Land

Just like the traditional home, you need a plot of land where you can build your container home.

In order to build a container home, you need a lot of space for storing the building materials, including the containers. You should have enough space to align the containers, usually double size of your containers and additional 10-20 ft. of space on your plot. The land where you are building your home should also be in level. There should be a good drainage system as well. Before you begin to stack containers, you should build a concrete foundation.

The Foundation Types

"Do I need a foundation?" you might ask.
The answer is: Yes, of course!

For better support, the foundations for your shipping container home should be made like the standard steel and concrete structure. Basically, there are three types of foundations:

- Deep basement
- Crawl space (strip foundation)
- Slab on grade (concrete piers)

A: DEEP BASEMENT   B: CRAWL SPACE   C: SLAB-ON-GRADE

What type of foundations you should use for your container home depends on various factors such as your building plans, the design, soil type and local climate.

Deep basement: You can place a container under the ground and stack another above it. You can then use the underground container as the basement. This type of foundation will give you a spacious storage and living space. You should still make a concrete pier foundation for the container that's underground. You should add pebbles under the container to make it easier for the water to flow away.

Crawl space: If you need extra storage or the land you are building on is sloped, you can go for this option. You can also make it completely go round and make a little door in it to store some stuff.

This method is preferred in colder climates because there is not much draft under the container, making your container more energy efficient by trapping the air under your container.

Traditional concrete block: This is the most common type of foundation. The container is stacked on the concrete foundation and welded to the embedded steel reinforcements.

The foundations for your container home has to follow the same protocol of the traditional home, however, you can forgo some codes. Just like in the traditional homes, you can have a crawl space and basement in your container home, however, the basic foundations should always be made from concrete and steel reinforcements.

Cutting windows and doors

One your containers are lined up and welded together, you can start with cutting windows and doors. When you are going to install windows and doors you need to cut out a piece of metal with a grinder, reciprocating saw or torch.

If you are going to cut sections out it's best to begin at the sides, go to the bottom and finish with the top. At the very last point when the metal is still one inch attached to the structure be very careful. Get someone to help you or kick with something from a distance. Always wear safety gear like safety glasses, cut resistant gloves and earplugs. Remove all items that can catch fire.

First of all, you need to know the dimensions of the window or door you are going to install. It makes it a lot easier to have the windows and doors already in your possession so you can measure them carefully.

You can use wood or galvanic steel to make frames. I prefer galvanic steel because it doesn't rot in bad weather. In case you are using wood, don't forget to give it a waterproof coating.

I don't like wooden frames because it feels cheap and doesn't last long.

Windows

Make sure to measure your windows from the outside so it starts on the same level of a ridge.

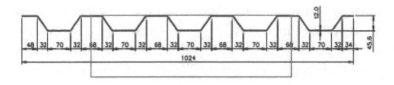

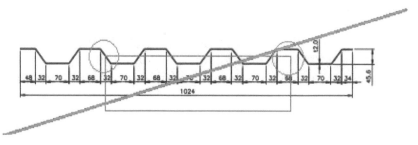

Firstly, make a galvanic steel frame around the window which you would like to install. If the frame is ready you can now measure the dimensions of the frame and mark it on the shipping container.

Make the cut in your container. Don't forget to clean the edges with a flapper disk.

Once you have a hole in your container you can spot weld the frame in place. It's better to spot weld on opposing sides (in the beginning) to prevent warping of the frame.

Now, finish the frame with anti-corrosion (spray) paint. Before placing the window in the frame use silicon around the edges to prevent water from coming in. Then place the window in the frame and weld or drill the window to the frame.

Doors

For the doors it's quite the same process. But this time you need it to rest at the bottom of the container. You don't need to have a full frame. You can leave the beam of the bottom part out and use the structure of the container.

Adding the door and finishing it off with silicone and anti-corrosion paint.

Flooring

The container floor is seaworthy, heavily treated 28mm thick plywood or bamboo. The container floor is usually made from birch, teak or keruing plywood laminates. The floor can withstand tons of weight, is very durable and resistant to water.

During the shipping, the floors are likely to be damaged. There could be cracks and missing layers.

If you want to smooth out the surface with a sander, always wear a mask with filter. This is because the particles that come from the floor can be toxic.

Personally, I like to use garage floor coating (suited for wood) to incapsulate the floor. This will also help in covering up chemicals that have been used to treat the floor.

If you are done with the treating of the floor you can start by putting in the framing. We will add insulation after the framing is done.

Add framing

One you have installed your windows and doors you can add the framing. Framing is not only used to make walls but it's also for running your electrical cables and water pipes trough. This way you can strategically locate your sockets and light switches.

As you can see in the previous picture, the wooden framing is placed around the windows.

Wooden framing is preferred because you don't want make "cold bridges" in your new home. When it's cold outside you don't want the cold air to come inside your container. The cold air gets "bridged" to the interior. Cold bridges are made when you use metal framing.

You have to adjust the depth and spacing of your frame work to the type and width of your insulation material. For example, you have fiberglass suited for 2 by 4-inch framing, you should suit your framing to 2 by 4inch insulation rolls.

If you want to hang things on the wall like kitchen cabinets, you need to add wooden cross pieces between the framing. This way you know when you are hanging something it is secure.

Before covering everything up after insulation be sure to note where the framing is. If you need to hang something up you can drill in the wooden frame and not in the electrical or plumbing.

Electrical and plumbing

After the framing is done you can install the electrical and plumbing.

Electrical

To install the electrical, you need to have one location for the main switchboard.

It's preferred to install the main switchboard in a place which you won't look at all the time. I would place it somewhere hidden but still accessible. If a fuse fails, you could simply open the switchboard and put it back on.

Once you are done drawing your electrical plan you need to mount all the boxes and switches to the desired location. Once all that is in place you can start by drilling holes in your framing to pull the cable trough. It might help to label the cables so you are not confused and don't change cables.

The recommended gauge for lighting is 14-gauge wire and a 15-amp circuit breaker.

The recommended gauge for power outlets is 12-gauge and a 20-amp circuit breaker.

Here is some math to calculate the number of watts that go through a wire:

Power = Voltage x Amps
We can draw this in a triangle:

P= Power (Watts)
V= Volts (Volt)
A= Amps (Amps)

Here are some formulas:
P= VxA
V= P/A
A= P/V

To determine how many sockets you can have on one fuse, you need to do some planning and calculation. What kind of appliance am I going to use for that socket? For example, if you are going to use an air conditioner, it's best to use one breaker for that appliance.

Let's do some math!
I have an air conditioner that draws 1920watts.

I would like to know the amps for this appliance. This is how to do it: Amps (A) is Power (P) divided by Volts (V).
(You can see it in the triangle)
A=P/V so, 1920watts/120 volts = 16amps.

My amperage is below 20amps so I can use the standard 20amp fuse for the socket. You probably have seen that there is 4 amps leftover. If you plug in another high-power appliance on the same fuse it will shut off. That's why you need several fuses and calculate what you are going to use for each socket. Generally, you could use 2-4 sockets for each breaker.

as for lights:

I have 4 led lights of 10Watts and 5 led lights of 15watts (assuming they are 120Volts). These lights combined will need 115watts. Now how many amps are that? A=P/V -> 115watts/120 volts= 0.95amps. You will note that this amperage is far les than our other example.

Lights demand less power than big appliances. So practically you could have more lights per breaker then sockets have outlets. But I would not advise to use only one breaker for all of the lights.

Imagine, one way or another the breaker shuts off. You will be left with no lights. It's better to have the lights on a separate breaker for each room or a couple of rooms. Not the whole house.

Here are some of the most common electrical uses you should take into consideration if you are mapping out the power and data for your container home.

- Lights
- Outlets
- Internet cable
- Tv cable
- Outdoor lights and outlets

Plumbing

The first question you should ask yourself is what kind of system do you want to use? Would you like and off-grid system or an on-grid system?

If you want an off-grid system you need to have a water collection system in place. If you have access to the grid you don't need any of these. There are different methods of plumbing available:

- Copper
- Cpdc
- Pex

Copper
Pros: soldered connections, long lasting
Cons: high cost, more skill is required

Cpdc
Pros: glued connection, relatively cheap
Cons: questionable with longevity

Pex
Pros: easy installation, each line can be individually shut off
Cons: not a glued or soldered connection

I would pick Pex over everything else. It's straight forward to install and each line can be shut off seperatly. This can be helpful when you are changing a faucet. It's much cheaper too. In my opinion Pex comes first, then copper and lastly Cpdc.

Always insulate your hot and cold lines. The pipes are close to the exterior wall. In order for your pipes not to freeze in cold temperatures you need to insulate. Also, you need to insulate against heat loss in your hot pipe. It will take longer for you to have hot water out of your faucet when your hot pipes are not insulated.

Hot water heaters

First of all, the placement is very important. You should place your water heater as close as possible to your bathroom, kitchen faucets or any other tap off point that requires hot water.

This is because when hot water sits in your pipes for a while it will cool down. If the water in these pipes are cooled down it will take longer for you to have hot water at your faucet. Ideal location of a heater should be between your bathroom and kitchen.

Should I use one with a reservoir or without one?

Reservoir
Pros: always have it available
Con: waste of space, using energy to keep it hot, when you are out of hot water it takes time to reheat.

No reservoir
Pros: Heats water very quickly. Not wasting energy like the tank version.
Con: when you run out of electricity or gas there is no hot water, takes a little bit longer to have hot water

Combination of a small tank and direct heater (one unit)
This is the best of both worlds if the space allows it. You will get hot water immediately from the small reservoir and the direct heater will provide you with more hot water after some time.

If space is a problem, go with the direct heater as close as possible to your faucets. If space is not a problem, go with the combination of a small tank and direct heater (one unit).

Now let's go over the different kinds of heating.

Propane heater
Pro: Less expensive then electricity, simple system, more efficient, less heavy on your electrical system.
Con: it shouldn't be installed in the same room with a gas stove.

Electrical heater
Pro: small, you can place it in your kitchen

Con: expensive if you don't have solar panels, not an efficient way of heating, more maintenance required then propane heaters.

I would go with a propane heater because it requires less maintenance then electric. Is easy to install and doesn't require a heavy electric circuit. This is also the go-to option if you are off the grid.

Here are some of the mostly used distribution points where you need hot and cold water.

- Kitchen sink
- Shower
- Bathroom sink
- Toilet
- Washroom

If you are done installing plumbing, you need to test it for any leaks. Pressurize the system for at least one day and check for any leaks. Don't do this when it's freezing because your lines will break.

After you have checked for leaks you can add the insulation.

Insulation and Weatherproofing

Containers are steel boxes; you need insulation to make them livable.

Why do you need insulation in the first place?

Heat Control: Since the containers are steel structures, they absorb and transmit heat and cold. The container cannot be controlled if no insulation is used.

Humidity: The moist of the interior air condenses against the cold steel. This will lead to condensation and after some time mold.

Temperature: Steel is a good conductor of heat and cold. Insulation is needed to make the containers appropriate for you to live comfortably in without outrageous energy bills.

You might be wondering what kind of insulation is ideal for your container home. The type of insulation you should use depends on various things such as:

- Cost involved
- Your local climate
- Environment friendliness

You not only need to insulate the inside of your container but painting the outside of your container can have a big difference.

If you live in a hot climate with the sun beating down on your house, you can consider ceramic insulation sprayed or painted on the outside of your container to reflect the heat. Ceramic paint has a good R-value.

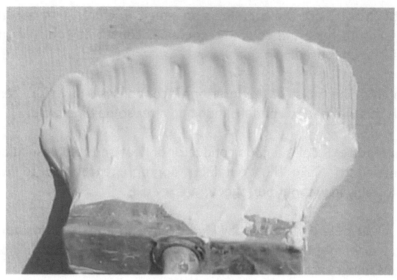
Ceramic paint

If you would like to go cheaper you can use white paint. I prefer using white paint over ceramic insulation because of the cost involved.

Don't make the mistake of painting your shipping container black if you live in a hot climate. You will basically create an oven.

Here are some insulation types you can consider for your container:

Fiberglass insulation (glass wool)
Fiberglass insulation is one of the common insulation methods in traditional homes. Fiberglass insulation is also widely used in container homes. The fiberglass is generally 3.5 inches thick and provides good protection against outside heat or cold and maintains indoor temperature. The fiberglass covers the ribbed sides of the walls as well as the electric wiring

If you don't wear protection it will irritate your skin, eyes and respiratory system. You need to know what you are doing If you are using fiberglass.

This insulation will come in rolls and depending on the type the fibers might be covered with paper (like packaging). Don't remove these, they will protect you from the fibers.

They can be hard to install if you are running quite a lot of electrical wires and plumbing trough the framing. You will have to install a moisture barrier if you use this insulation.

You will need to install a vapor barrier (more in this later). It has an R-value of 3.5 per inch.

Styrofoam insulation

It's also called blue board or close-cell extruded polystyrene foam (XPS). It's different from the classic white foam you see in packaging. This is because the white foam is expanded while the blue Styrofoam is extruded. Its R-value is 5 per inch.

If you want to install Styrofoam into your framing, you need to finish the corners off with a spray foam can to seal the edges.

If you decide to go with Styrofoam, be prepared to cut a lot of boards because the boards won't fit the frames most of the times.

As like fiberglass insulation it's quite hard and a lot of work to install Styrofoam along your walls. That's why I'm going to talk more about spray foam next. You will have to install a moisture barrier if you use this insulation.

Styrofoam insulation

Spray Foam
Spray foam also provides good insulation to container homes. The spray foam completely hides the ribs, plumbing and electrical wiring. Unlike fiberglass or polystyrene panels, spray foam does not leave any gaps between the wall and insulation. Therefore, there is no chance of condensation or moisture developing.

The open cell variant provides and R-3,5 value

The closed cell variant provides an R-6 value per inch. It's more expensive than the open cell but has a great advantage besides it having a better R value then open cell.

Let's say you are using open spray foam and its very cold outside (freezing). You are sitting cozy in your seat at room temperature. The air inside has more vapor in it than the cold air outside. Because the cells of the spray foam are open and not closed the warm air touches the cold surface and starts to condensation. Leading to rust and rotting.

If you would have used closed foam spray the air from the inside can't reach the outer wall because it's air tight. So, no condensation would form against the wall of your container.

So, if you decide to use open spray foam you need to install a vapor barrier which is situated between your framing and the drywall. It's not easy to seal everything. Personally, I wouldn't take the risk to use open foam because the chances of rotting are present. You are better of using closed spray foam and paying a little more (if you live in a cold climate).

Closed Cell	Open Cell
Cold climates	Warm climates
Strong and firm	Weaker
Air barrier at 1.5"	Air barrier at 3.5"
Moisture barrier at 1.5"	No moisture barrier
R-6 per inch	R-3.5 per inch
Costs more	Costs less

Open cell can be beneficial in hot climates. Open cell has the ability to breathe. So, if there is a leak somewhere it will evaporate back trough the ceiling or wall. The only works if there is a vapor barrier.

Spray foam can also be used as a thin layer (1.5 inch) to stop condensation to form on the inner walls. If the thin layer has been sprayed on you can add other types of insulation like rockwool, fiberglass or others.

This is a table for the recommended R-value in your home depending on the climate and your heating system. You will note that the R value for your ceiling is recommended to be the highest. That's because heat transfers more easily trough the sealing then the walls.

Regional R-Values

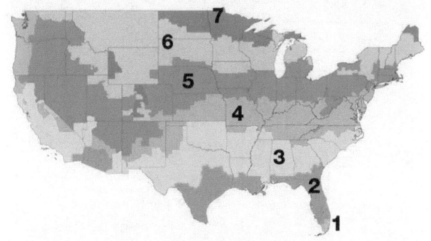

The Department of Energy recommends different insulation levels based on regional climate zones to increase energy efficiency

Zone	Attic	WALLS 2x4	2x6	Floors	Crawlspaces
7	R49 to R60	R13 to R15	R19 to R21	R25 - R30	R25 to R30
6	R49 to R60	R13 to R15	R19 to R21	R25 - R30	R25 to R30
5	R38 to R60	R13 to R15	R19 to R21	R25 - R30	R25 to R30
4	R38 to R60	R13 to R15	R19 to R21	R25 - R30	R25 to R30
3	R30 to R60	R13 to R15	R19 to R21	R25	R19 to R25
2	R30 to R49	R13 to R15	R19 to R21	R13	R13 to R19
1	R30 to R49	R13 to R15	R19 to R21	R13	R13

For example, you live in zone 4. You will need a minimum of R-38 for the ceiling, R13 for the walls and 25 for the floor. You will need:

	R-Value (per inch)	Ceiling	Walls	Floors
Fiberglass	3.5	10.9	3.7	
Styrofoam	5.0	7.6	2.6	5.0
Open cell spray foam	3.5	10.9	3.7	
Closed cell spray foam	6.0	6.3	2.2	

We will only use Styrofoam as insulation for floors. Read more on this later.

You can use a mix of different types of insulation. You can choose Styrofoam paneling for the roof, spray foam for the walls and Styrofoam paneling for the floor.

Venting

You can use the existing vents in the container to create airflow. You need to make a box around it to it's not obstructed by insulation.

If you prefer your own venting system you need to get rid of these vent's. It's advised to use silicone to cover up the vent. If it's hot outside but colder on the inside moist air will get inside and create mold and rot if you don't cover these up.

Existing vent holes in the container

Adding floor insulation

After you have applied a coating to the floor, framed the interior, installed the electrical, plumbing and added insulation, it's time to add floor insulation.

While you can add spray foam on the underside of the container I don't recommend this because I haven't seen anybody do it.

What I do recommend is that you use insulation of about ¾ inch rigid foam insulation and cover it with sub flooring (wooden panels). Both the insulation and sub flooring should be tung and groove.

The reason why we add flooring after the framing is because the frame is mounted on the already existing floor. Which makes it a lot stronger.

Imagine we would screw the framing into the sub flooring and the rigid foam insulation panels. I won't be very strong. Plus, it would create cold bridges (metal screws) and we don't want that.

After you have installed the water lines, done the electrical and finished with adding insulation it's time to add drywall and start painting.

In the next chapter we will talk about adding a roof to your container home. It's not necessary but it looks good and can be used as a storage space if needed.

Roofing

The recommended weight for the roof itself is just 300 kg. But you can stack 8 containers on top of each other. This is because the skeleton is very strong but the roof itself, connecting the skeleton is weak.

You can install a roof on your container. But most people go without installing a roof because they see this as a way to cut building cost. One thing to keep in mind is snow. If you have a lot of snow and can't clear it yourself, you will need a sloped roof or a reinforced roof that build on top of the container skeleton.

If you have decided to install a roof, here are a few various considerations for different roof styles:

Shed roof
The shed style roof is basically a sloped roof. Many people use this style roof because it is cheap, simple to build and takes a short time to install. There is also another advantage of shed style roof. You can install solar panels easily.

The shed style roof is installed by building a truss. The truss is built by welding steels across the container and covering with shingles, galvanized metal sheets or coated steel sheets. You also need to cover the truss with bracing in order to protect from strong wind.

If you enclose it like the picture below you can have extra storage space.

Shed roof

Gable roof

Many people go with gable style because gable style roof is normally associated with traditional home and by having gable roof, you can style your container home as a traditional home. The gable roof has a unique triangle look. This type of roof will not hold as much snow as a shed roof, thus making it lighter. A gable roof also creates more space in the ceiling, depending on the angle of course.

First of all, you need to build a truss by welding steel on your container, and then you need to cover the roof creating slopes on both sides. You can use shingles, galvanized metal sheets or coated steel sheets to cover the roof.

Gable roof

Cool Design Ideas

Throughout the world, shipping containers have been used to build different kinds of structures. A simple Google search will show you what can be built from shipping containers. The following list will give you a basic idea of what the alternative uses of shipping containers are.

Shipping containers are used to create:

- Affordable housing
- Emergency hurricane shelters for thoroughbred horses
- Fire training facility
- Military training facility
- Emergency shelters
- School buildings
- Apartment and office buildings

- Artists' studios
- Stores
- Moveable exhibition spaces on rails
- Radar stations
- Sleeping rooms
- Recording studios
- Modular data centers
- Experimental labs
- Combatant temporary containment
- Bathrooms
- Workshops
- Hotels/Hostels
- Mine site accommodations
- Food trucks
- Storage for farms
- Battery storage units

A popular use of shipping containers is the Starbucks store in Broadway, Chicago.

3. Moving into a Container Home

You need various kinds of utilities such as gas, water, and electricity in your home. Installing utilities in a container home is just like installing utilities in any traditional home. You can restrict plumbing in one, two or three locations (kitchen, dining room and bathroom) and minimize the cost. Installing gas in the kitchen is as simple as installing gas in a traditional home.

You can even go creative by installing solar panels on the roof and produce your own electricity or have solar water heater. If you do not want to incorporate solar panels or a solar water heater right away, you can always install it later. You need to keep in mind that you can upgrade, so you need to make it easy to attach to your current system.

If you do not have a civic water supply in your location, you can install water tanks and begin harvesting rainwater.

Legal Protection

Just like with traditional home building, shipping container homes also require a building permit. However, if you happen to be located outside the zoning area, you may not need to follow building codes. You should always stay safe by checking the building codes in your area. Building codes are different in different areas.
You also need insurance for your container home. Since container homes are earthquake and hurricane proof, getting insurance will not be that difficult.

Interior Designs

In this chapter you can get some inspiration of other designs. You can check online to see how a finished container looks like. You may not even recognize it as a shipping container when exterior finishes are done.

Another question that you might face is: are container homes tall enough to comply with the building codes? The general requirement of a home is 8 feet tall. This is the standard height of a residential home. The shipping containers have 8.6 feet height. You even have a better option to make your home taller by getting HC containers which are about 12 feet tall.

The following designs are not mine, so I don't take credit for them. I do like them and I wanted to share them with you.

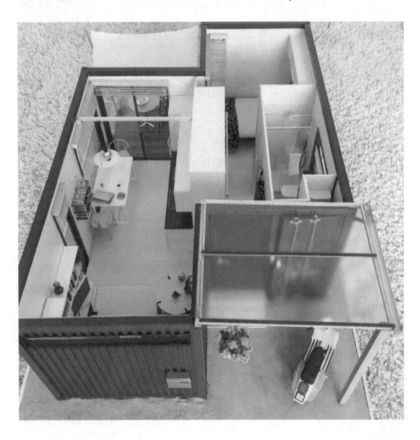

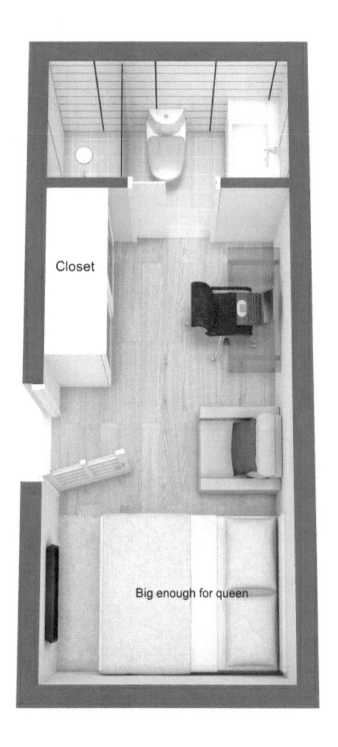

Closet

Big enough for queen

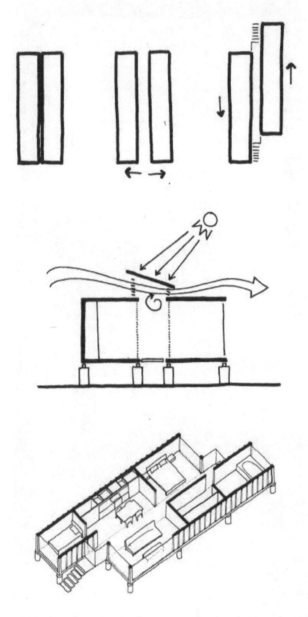

In the image above, four containers are set to have a gap between them. When the sun creates heat on the top panel draft will take over and create natural ventilation.

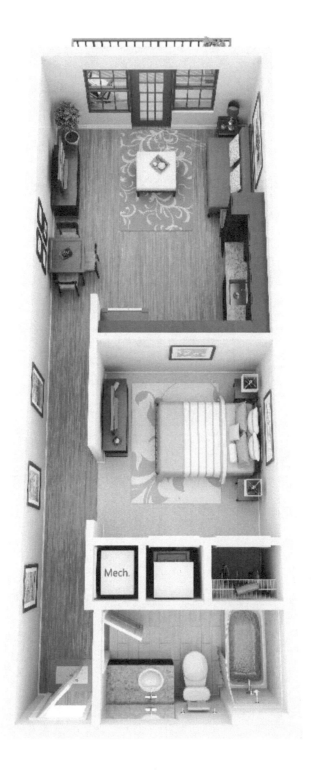

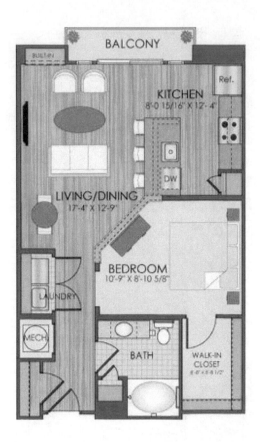

BALCONY

BUILT-IN

KITCHEN
8'-0 15/16" X 12'- 4"

Ref.

DW

LIVING/DINING
17'-4" X 12'-9"

BEDROOM
10'-9" X 8'-10 5/8"

LAUNDRY

MECH.

BATH

WALK-IN
CLOSET
6'-6" x 5'-6 1/2"

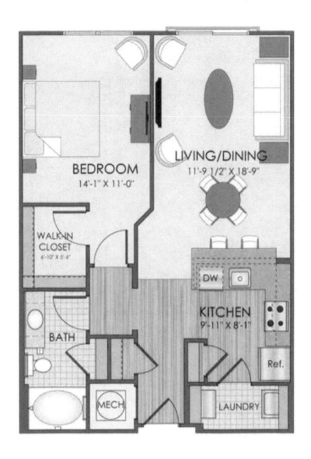

BEDROOM
14'-1" X 11'-0"

LIVING/DINING
11'-9 1/2" X 18'-9"

WALK-IN
CLOSET
6'-10" X 5'-6"

BATH

KITCHEN
9'-11" X 8'-1"

DW

Ref.

MECH

LAUNDRY

LIVING
19'-5 1/2" X 10'-5 1/8"

BEDROOM
12'-0" X 11'-9"

KITCHEN
10'-3" X 8'-8"

CLOSET
5'-7" X 5'-3"

DW

Ref.

BATH

DINING
10'-11 1/4" X 8'-11 7/8"

LAUNDRY

FOYER

MECH

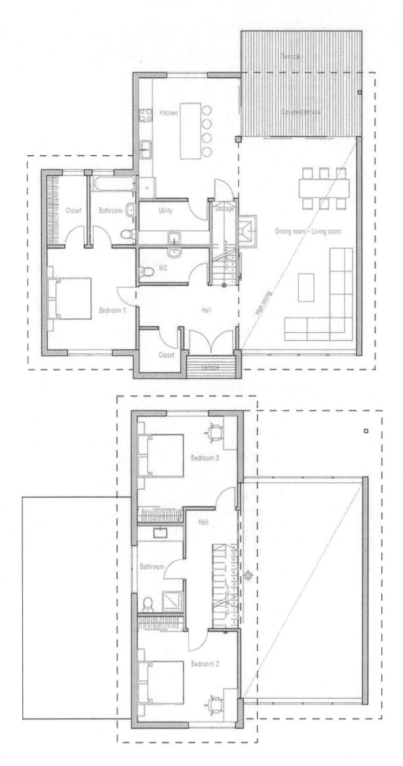

Kitchen

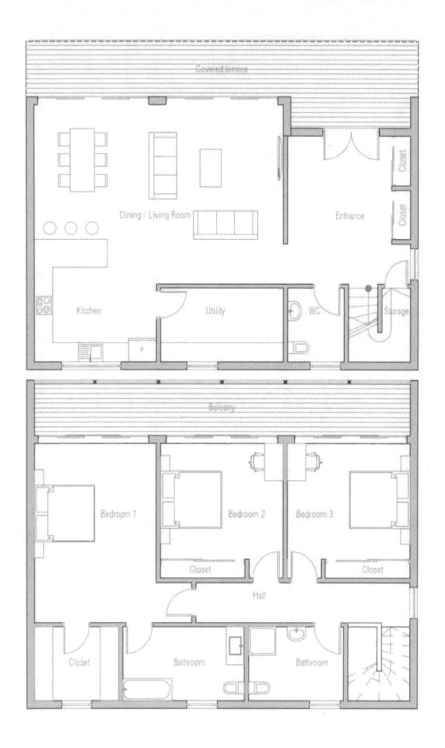

Covered terrace

Closet

Closet

Dining / Living Room

Entrance

Kitchen

Utility

WC

Storage

Balcony

Bedroom 1

Bedroom 2

Bedroom 3

Closet

Closet

Closet

Hall

Closet

Bathroom

Bathroom

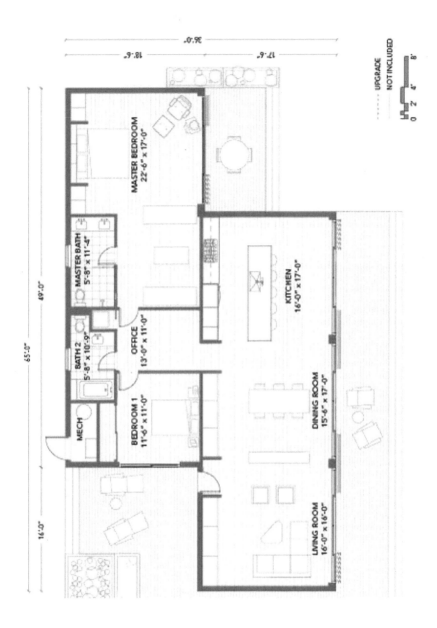

MASTER BEDROOM
22'-6" x 17'-0"

MASTER BATH
5'-8" x 11'-4"

BATH 2
5'-8" x 10'-9"

OFFICE
13'-0" x 11'-0"

BEDROOM 1
11'-6" x 11'-0"

MECH

KITCHEN
16'-0" x 17'-0"

DINING ROOM
15'-6" x 17'-0"

LIVING ROOM
16'-0" x 16'-0"

36'-0"

18'-6"

17'-6"

49'-0"

65'-0"

16'-0"

UPGRADE

NOT INCLUDED

0 2 4'   8'

71

20' "STACKER"

HOT WATER

PANTRY

REF.

BATH

COMPOSTING
TOILET

WASHER
DRYER

RANGE

SINK

ENTRY

DAYBED
SEATING

PULL OUT TABLE

1 METER
STAIRCASE

CORNER
MEDIA CTR.

LINEN

SINK

BATH

STO

QUEEN BED
PEDESTAL STO.

STEP UP

1 METER
STAIRCASE

CLOSET

DECK

72

40' Container Home

40' Container
Camp Cabin

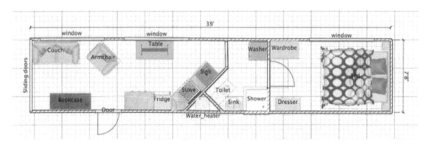

40' Container Home

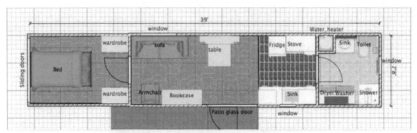

40' Container Home

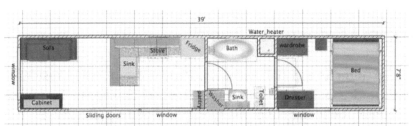

40' Container Home

Crucial Mistakes to Avoid

Cargo architecture is on the rising. People are building residential homes, office buildings, local businesses, shopping malls, schools, community buildings and many other building structures from shipping containers. Since containers are strong and easy to customize, they are well suited for any kind of structures.

However, things are not so simple. Building with shipping containers still has many challenges. One of the major problems associated with building with shipping containers is the absence of experts as the idea is still new.

If you are serious about building shipping containers, here are some crucial mistakes you should avoid.

- Whether you are buying a used container or one-trip container, make sure to check the containers you are buying.

- Used containers are cheap and they still have decades of life left. However, consider investing in a one-trip container. You will never repent of extra investment.

- For hassle free building and any legal complications that you might have later, check the building permits in your area.

- If you do not have experience, you probably need a contractor. While looking for a contractor, try to find a contractor that can give you a finished home, instead of hiring multiple contractors for the building and interior designing.

- Generally, shipping containers are 8.6 feet tall. However, you can find 12 feet tall container. It's better to get a high cube container. Especially if you live in colder climates (insulation).

- You should understand the shipping container's structure beforehand so that you do not come across problems during the customization of the containers.

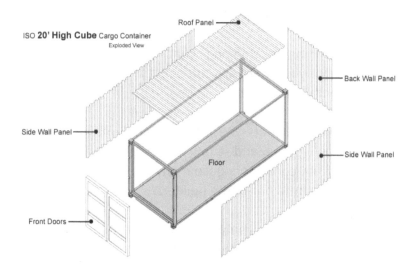

- Building with containers saves you money, but don't expect to make huge savings.

- You need to cut and weld while modifying the containers. It is time-consuming. Learn how to minimize the required welding.

- Containers need to be insulated before you can move in. Find out various insulation methods and always use the method that is durable and cost-effective for your climate.

- Consider what kind of utilities are must. Plan plumbing, electrical wiring, beforehand.

- Use personal protection when you are working. Use gloves, hearing protection, a hard hat and safety glasses.

Is a Shipping Container Home for You?

So you are planning a shipping container home, is shipping container home for you? Here are some myths and facts associated with shipping container homes.

Some of the obvious benefits of using containers to build homes are saving money, saving time, and strong and durable home. However, building homes from containers pose many questions and concerns from the potential container-home builders.

You might be one of those who wants to build a shipping container home but confused about whether it is right for you or not. One of the questions that might be bothering you could be: how could I build my dream home within the seemingly-obvious limitations of using metal containers?

Here are some myths and facts that will clear the misconceptions about container-homes:

A lot of people are attracted to shipping container homes because you can save a lot of money on construction material. Since the basic structure is already present, you don't need walls, floors, even roofs to build. This saves at least 30 percent in construction cost (depending on what container you get).

Using containers as building materials also saves money on weather-proofing and exterior cladding. When you are using containers, your per square cost will also substantially reduce.

Apart from building cost, you can also save building time. The basic structure is already present and all you have to do is some modifications to walls, windows, doors, and insulation. Construction time can be cut down.

But there is a flip side. Building a shipping container home saves time and money might be a one-sided view. You can, of course, get a shipping container for $1500-$3500, however, you need at least three containers to make a proper home for your family of 4. Shipping the huge metal boxes to your location adds to your construction cost. A lot of cutting and welding is required, which also makes building costly.

Many people are attracted towards container homes because they consider it easy building, which happens to be one of the myths of shipping container homes. If you do not have any prior experience, you might need a contractor. Hiring a contractor to build your shipping home can cost as much as building a traditional home. You might need a contractor to finish the building and another to do the interior.

Following regulations can also be a headache. Every state/country has its own sets of rules and standards, which means a container house in the US does not look like a container house in the UK.

Since containers are steel boxes designed to stand harsh sea weather, container homes are strong and durable. They are considered 10 times stronger than the traditional homes in times of earthquakes and hurricanes.

For a green and sustainable living, container homes are better solutions. According to a rough estimate, there are around 24 million unused shipping containers on earth. Generally, containers are retired after only 10 to 15 years use, however, they can last more than that, even for decades. Reusing these containers means you are saving resources.

Other things to consider:

- The land should not be soggy when the truck comes to deliver the container.
- Is it possible to connect the container home to the grid? Electricity, water and sewage.
- If you want internet, are you able to stay with your current provider?
- How would you manage garbage? Is there a garbage truck passing your property?

Risks Involved

Throughout the book, we have devoted chapters on the advantages of building with shipping containers and how beneficial is it use shipping containers as a home.

However, container homes also have many disadvantages.
I want to conclude the book with some of the major disadvantages of building shipping container homes.

Lack of flexibility
You can, of course, stack containers or align containers, to build big homes. However, the process is very long and tedious. Lack of flexibility is one of the major drawbacks of building with containers. Moving 20 or 40 feet long steel boxes in the residential area can be difficult. You also need a lot of space to park the containers while building the house.

You need a crane or forklift to stack or align the containers, which is time-consuming and costly.

Cargo spillages and solvents

Containers are used to ship a wide variety of materials. They might have been used to ship materials that are hazardous to human health. Due to spillage, the containers can be contaminated. You need to clean thoroughly before you can make it a home.

Building cost

Of course, you save money if you build with shipping containers. However, your building cost can rise and might even cost you as much as building a traditional house. You need specialized labor to cut and weld the steel frames.

4. Recommendations

First of all, I would like to thank you for getting my book on building container homes. The Idea of this book was to give you an impression on what's involved and determining of this is something for you. I hope I have fulfilled this and give you some valuable tips you can use later on.

There is only so much you can get from a book. Sometimes it's better to actually see people doing it on video. That's why I have compiled a list of YouTube channels where people are building their own container house or are exploring other's people container house. Enjoy!

- Paul Chambers's channel on YouTube
- Julian Goulding's channel on YouTube
- Container Acre on YouTube
- Odd Life Crafting on YouTube
- Kirsten Dirksen her channel on YouTube

If you decide to build your own container home, do not forget to take pictures, film it or even make video's like the YouTube channels mentioned. It will make building with shipping containers more popular and accepted.

Happy Building!

Made in United States
Troutdale, OR
01/08/2025

27750328R00050